I Could Be Worse

I Could Be Worse

Based on a true story

Larissa Clark

Table of Contents

Prologue: Life How I Knew It

Chapter 1: Rainbows and Sunshine

Chapter 2: Take the Stand

Chapter 3: The Dark Road Alone

Chapter 4: I'm Doing Great, Thanks for Asking

Chapter 5: Dear God, Are You There?

Chapter 6: Love is an Illusion

Chapter 7: The Big Break Up

Chapter 8: Being a Mom and Living with Trauma

Acknowledgements

  Being vulnerable and publishing a book about my life was the biggest accomplishment I have ever completed in my life. There are so many people that played a part in my journey that led me to writing this book. I am truly humbled for the specific individuals who helped me throughout the writing and publishing process.
  I am forever indebted to my editor, Ursula Squire and my graphics designer, Danica Calvert, who worked diligently on this project. Thank you for continuously holding me accountable, especially in those challenging moments when I would get frustrated writing the book. It is because of your efforts and keen insight that my voice can be heard and can help other people who are struggling with their everyday life.
  I am sincerely grateful for my coach, Mark Wiggins, who educated me on the book process and coached me through the process step by step. I am grateful you have been brought into my life and pushed me to make an idea become a reality. A special thanks goes to my mentor, Mark Perry, who has been by my side supporting me. Thank you for always encouraging me to continue doing what I am passionate about, even though I wanted to give up and always giving constructive criticism.
  To all my friends and family, who have celebrated me on this long-awaited accomplishment and ongoing support throughout my journey, thank you for everything you do. I want to give a huge thank you to my number one supporter throughout my whole life, my mom. I know this

journey hasn't been easy for you and I can only imagine what it feels like for a parent to watch their child, but I am so blessed to have you as my mother because of how strong you are and that you continue to love me flaws and all. To my sister Kiaura: thank you for listening to my late-night FaceTime rambling sessions for the book and for also holding me accountable to stay focused and not procrastinate.

    Publishing this book couldn't have been possible without the key person. My former therapist, who introduced me to a new form of therapy and challenged me to process internal issues that have been negatively affecting my life all these years.

Prologue: Life How I Knew It

Even though he was very hard on me throughout my childhood, I continued to idolize him. I tried so hard to gain his approval and did what I could to make him proud. I grew up in a broken home, as a lot of children do these days. A common story of infidelity, which forced my parents to eventually go their separate ways. Unfortunately for me, I got the short end of the stick. Not only did I grow up with a distant father, but I also grew up with my stepdad, Kent, who treated me a way that no child should ever be treated. All I ever wanted was to be my daddy's little girl and did everything I could to gain his approval in order to make that dream come true. It makes me really appreciate the active dads that are in their children's lives consistently, rather than circumstantially.

Over the years I have been carrying a heavy burden of being a disappointment to my dad and other people because I believe that I'm not good enough for them to be proud of me or want to accept me. Up until recently I have taken the next big step on processing what all my past and present relationships have matured into and that I have always had my expectations of others held too high. I was so desperate for approval and love that I swallowed a lot of secrets and swore I would take them to my grave with me when I died. Even till this day, I struggle opening up and being vulnerable to people because I feel that I have failed as a daughter, as a friend, as a partner, as a mother, and as a sister.

My dad has always shown love, though he has always used the *tough love* tactic, which I wasn't able to connect with and was very uninviting to me. I've always wondered if he feels responsible for what happened to me, or does he feel like he failed me as a father? There was a lot of change in my eighth-grade year because of what happened, so I made the decision to move in with my dad who lived in Colorado Springs at the time. This was a very devastating time for my whole family. I do remember my father's approach on the situation made me feel like I was just another one of his mess-up students at the facility he used to work at. To him, I was just another sad story, and he always had the positive outlook that I would work through my issues and be normal because people go through it every day. That's his approach to everything.

    I felt like I was damaged goods. I carry that heavy weight on my shoulders today as I'm writing this book; I feel he didn't view me as his little girl anymore. I still have thoughts in the back of my head wondering if he is proud of me with the life I lived so far – or am I a major disappointment and embarrassment to him because I didn't turn out the way I was supposed to and instead I jeopardized his image?

Living with my dad was fine – I was excited to finally be given the opportunity to get closer to him. That's when I started going to counseling. My therapist at the time was very nice we did a lot of hands on activities to work through emotion and feeling. Our sessions ended when I moved back to Denver with my mom after school had ended for summer break.

There is still something that isn't being confronted and it is straining our relationship that stems from the past, which has been affecting me immensely and has forced us to grow apart. I aim to improve my emotional communication skills once I have processed my trauma more.

My relationship with my mother has been very challenging through the years after my abuse was revealed. I wasn't the easiest child to raise and once she discovered my abuse the dynamic of our relationship shifted. I have put my mother through a lot of hardships over the years; even when my abuse came to an end our relationship was difficult to maintain.

My therapy has focused largely on overcoming my trauma by reliving it. But through this comes healing. And through this healing it is essential that I recognize that my value is my own. Not something anyone can take away from me. It also has taught me how to process these feelings. As my adult years have unfolded, I have realized the love that I need to feel comes from *within* me. My worth is not dependent on any man, any other person, besides myself.

A Note for the Reader:

This is a book about trauma. But more importantly, it is a book about how the trauma provided the ashes through which I will rise. The book serves two purposes: an account of my experience, and an account of my growth.

This isn't a story written just for you to feel sorry for me. This a story to see how I learned self- awareness from many of my life experiences. It's a story of knowing when to ask for help from the ones I love and trust. It's a story of outreach towards survivors battling with trauma and in hopes will learn that **YOU ARE NOT ALONE**.

This journey consists of fighting for life, learning how to forgive, and not letting my traumatic experiences dictate my well-being, but instead use what happened to me for the better.

I Could Be Worse

1.

Sunshine and Rainbows

January 31, 2004

"Dear diary,
today I am on my way to Texas then to Colorado. Mom is down at Colorado with Kiaura. I have been waiting for this day for a very long time. I'm in Louisiana and almost to Texas. I am so bored Mr. Kent keeps ignoring me I think he hates me after what I said last night. That's okay he can hate me forever. I won't be honest to him anymore and won't talk to him. He makes me so mad. I always have my mom I DON'T NEED HIM ANYMORE."

-Larissa Clark

Kent always made me feel comfortable enough to confide in him about anything, even more than my mom did. I was six years old when he came into my life. Kent was really nice to me, which made me warm up to him fairly easy. My mom and I were living in Denver at the time when he started coming around more frequently. On a spring afternoon Kent and I were at my house while my mom was at work. It was the perfect opportunity where I could confide in him about a sexual pleasure I had accidentally discovered. That pleasurable feeling made me feel good but was such a foreign feeling that I felt obligated to talk to someone I trusted about what I had done.

  I walked up to him and told him with uncertainty because I still couldn't understand why the water made me feel that way. Instead of him handling the situation in an adult manner, he used it to his advantage and wanted me to repeat the act, but this time while watching me. As a six-year-old I thought his reaction was innocent, but later learned he was grooming me. Over the course of time the grooming phase advanced into something much bigger.

My mom and Kent's relationship grew stronger and transitioned into a heavily committed relationship. The strength of their relationship and new job opportunities allowed us to uproot from Denver to Marietta, Georgia when I was 7 years old. By this time, Kent had become the ultimate manipulator and continued to push the boundaries in our relationship to see what he could get away with. He introduced me to pornographic movies, which was so foreign to me and made me feel very uncomfortable. Once he realized I was acclimated to watching pornography with him, he took things to the next level. He casually made me take my pants off and lay on the bed, then demanded me to cover my eyes. It hurt so bad I remember crying but was instructed to not open my eyes during that time or I would get in trouble.

Being touched in all different places of my body transitioned into receiving oral sex while covering my eyes. He always made the effort to have a blanket/towel over his head so I couldn't see what he was physically doing to me. During the time I was only allowed to look at the pornographic videos that were playing on the television, but eventually the acts advanced into penetration while covering my eyes. Within a matter of months Kent was having sexual intercourse with me, making me perform oral sex and receive oral sex all while my mom wasn't around.

I started developing behavioral issues and acting out in school. Nobody could understand why I was being so defiant and misbehaving, especially since I was always a bubbly child. It even got to a point where I was displaying sexual acts on my Barbie dolls in front of my classmates. I guess that is a good way to know that something may be wrong in a seven-year-old child's life.

Having me at his disposal wasn't good enough for Kent, the sex acts evolved into a punishment option whenever I got into trouble. He gave me a choice to either get whooped with a leather belt while stripped naked or have sex with him. Obviously, I chose the second option because it ended quicker and it wouldn't leave bruises, welts, or puncture my skin afterward.

As I got older, the sex acts gradually became more frequent – it didn't even matter if we were traveling, or on family vacations, even on road trips – he would always find a way to be alone with me and take advantage of my body.

When I was going on eleven years old, we relocated back to Denver. My mom had gotten hired for a new job and was already out there getting our living situation situated. Before she left for Colorado, I begged to go with her but they both said no because I had to go to school and help Kent with the rest of the move. Our truck was finally packed, and we were on our way to our new home in Denver, Colorado. Late that night Kent decided to pull the truck over because he claimed to be tired, but he attempted to make me give him oral sex while my little sister was in the backseat sleeping. I politely declined and came up with a clever excuse so he wouldn't take matters into his own hands. In moments like those I really enjoyed writing my thoughts in my diary.

Unfortunately, I had to be cautious and conservative what I wrote in my diary. Kent tended to go through my diary entries and tear out any pages he didn't approve of, so eventually the writing came to a complete stop. Creating song lyrics and poetry was a new outlet that I turned to for coping. I learned to express my pain through music and poetic lyric, until he found those to and discarded them, leaving me with nothing but the sounds of music.

I got my first iPod in 2006. It was the new black 5th generation with 50 Gb. This was the greatest gift I could get because now I could escape from the hell I was living in, through the music playing in my ears. The first song I bought from my iTunes store was Runaway Love by Ludacris feat. Mary J Blige, which if either of you are reading this thank you for creating that song.

That song helped me get through many long painful nights and helped me not feel alone. I would listen to that song so much that it ended up being the most played song on my playlist. I would frequently cry myself to sleep at night while listening to that song on repeat. Ludacris was talking to me; he knew what I was going through. "*…Part of her is missin and nobody will listen… Sneaking in her room when her mommas knocked out, tryna have his was* *and little Lisa says ouch. She tries to resist, but all he does is beat her... Lisa's stuck up in the world on her own forced to think that hell is a place that's called home..."*

Some nights I would have to hurry and hide my iPod under my pillow and pretend that I was sleeping when Kent crept into my room. I would cringe when I felt his hard callus hands caressing my body. Even though I laid there and didn't respond, he would still work his hands down to my panties and proceed to have his way with me. During the many times he was having sex with me I would have to hide my tears running down my face. I'll never forget the grunts he always made while rocking back and forth on top of me. That's when I started unconsciously teaching myself how to disassociate. It was the only way I could survive through those horrid moments and it happened so often that I began to feel emotionally numb. It grew to a point where I was just existent in this world and living day to day.

Luckily, I ended up discovering a new coping outlet besides music. After watching the first episode of *Law and Order: SVU* I was hooked. I couldn't stop watching it. Finally, something that I could relate to and get a chance to escape from my real horror. Little did I know that Olivia Benson and her team were teaching me how to get out and do it in a strategic manner. *Law and Order: SVU* saved my life (literally) and educated me about sexual abuse and what it stands for. I quickly learned what Kent was doing to me was not okay and fathers don't have sex with their daughters.

With everything my mom was juggling she had no idea what Kent was doing to me. I watched her be a full-time mother of four, work long hours, and have a husband who wasn't entirely helpful, even though he could manage a secret life. She started traveling more for work and visiting family, she was in the hospital a couple of times giving birth to my siblings, and even when she went to her 5:00 AM gym workouts he would manage to slip into my room before I had to get up for school. Kent took advantage of those moments when my mom wasn't around during the day, but it occurred mostly in the evening when the house was silent, and everyone was asleep.

No matter what I did I wasn't safe – even when my mother was in the hospital having her third child. I begged and pleaded to go to the hospital and stay there, but he told me I had to stay at home. When he returned late that night from seeing my mom, he told me to take a shower with him so he could wash me. Afterward he made me perform oral sex, which led to having sex with me. You would think afterward I'd be released to go to my bedroom and go to sleep, but no – I had to sleep with him naked since my mom wasn't coming home. I felt like his personal sex slave, some nights he would be gentle and other nights I would feel like I was a prostitute.

The sex sessions with Kent became more frequent and wasn't a punishment option anymore. I watched him become greedier and bolder. It started out being weekly then escalated to everyday, and there was nowhere to run because we lived in the same house. Opportunities to be alone with me increased over time for many different reasons. At night when my mother was sleeping, he would sneak out of their room and creep into my bedroom to "sleep" with me because she was snoring too loud. We lived in a 5-bedroom house with couple of vacant beds available, he persisted on sleeping with me and made sure my mom didn't find out. I wanted to tell her so bad, but I knew he would kill me. By the grace of God, she found out anyway. She was livid and confronted him about it. She told him to not sleep with me anymore, there are other beds in the house. He disregarded what she said and continued to sleep with me but made sure this time he didn't get caught.

As I was getting older, I became more defiant towards him and started testing my boundaries. He was losing control over me, so he started threatening my life with loaded guns targeted at my head and I would get blows to the face whenever I resisted him. I was able to build up my confidence to confront Kent and ask what would happen if I told, since all those years he constantly reminded me that what he was doing was okay and I will thank him one day for teaching me how to make my future husband happy in the bedroom.

With the blank look in his eyes he shuffled to the hallway closet and grabbed one of his hunting rifles. He turned around and walked towards me while cocking the gun back. As I was standing eye to eye with the gun, he said to me, "If you ever tell anyone I will kill you myself and bury your body in the backyard. No one will ever come looking for you because I will tell them you ran away."

I felt the tears gliding down my cheeks and heard my heart racing in anticipation of what was going to happen next. That is when I knew he was serious. I looked up from the barrel of the gun and glared him in the eyes daring him to pull the trigger. That was the day I knew I was in a life or death situation. I didn't want to be in my body nor alive anymore. I felt trapped and no one could hear me. That was the start of the end... as time went by, I got smarter.

First attempt: When I got home from school, I heard Kent upstairs caring for my little brother, I walked swiftly to our medicine cabinet in the kitchen and found the Advil capsules. I ingested a handful of Advil pills, then hurried to the cleaning supplies and took a big chug of Pine sol. Yes, the cleaning supply. Shortly afterward he came downstairs and I instantly ran into the bathroom and started projectile vomiting in the toilet. He was standing in the doorway holding my little brother yelling at me about being pregnant. He proceeded to tell me I am a whore for sleeping around with all these guys at school and it wouldn't be his baby. Mind you I'm in 8th grade; having sex with any boy was out of the question. As I was dry heaving over the toilet, all I could do was sob while internalizing these cruel accusations he was saying to me.

    I was at my wit's end and since suicide didn't work maybe killing him would. I thought long and hard about this and had to get out of this hell I was living in every day. I went to the kitchen while everyone was asleep and grabbed the largest knife that was in the knife holder. I quietly went upstairs and crept into my parents' bedroom. I walked up to their bed and stood over Kent as he was sound asleep. I could hear my mother breathing heavily on the other side of him. I held the knife over him while standing in the dark contemplating on what I was going to do next. With rage in my eyes, I slowly lowered the knife to my side. Tears flooded my eyes and I quietly backed out of the room. I returned the knife in its rightful place and went back to my bed. I laid there angry with myself and full of guilt for not following through with my plan.

    Still feeling trapped and not knowing what to do, cutting my flesh was the next best thing in attempt to relieve the inner pain and anger. It wasn't satisfying enough and the anger was still growing, eventually I started throwing valuable objects throughout our house when no one was home hoping to break them and hoping Kent would notice.

    My parents hired a nanny that would come over during the day to watch my three younger siblings since Kent was going back to work and I was at school. Early one morning I was waiting for Kent to call my name so I could claim my punishment for getting caught sneaking my cell phone and texting a boy late the night before. Kent made me go into the basement so he could discipline me his way before he left work and our nanny arrived.

    After stepping off the last step in the basement, he made me strip down to my bare skin and started beating me all over my body with a leather belt. At a point I tried to fight back and that's when things escalated. With fire in his eyes, he started punching and hitting me like he was in a boxing match with a grown man. But that wasn't good enough for him, he then proceeded to tie the leather belt around my neck and gripped it so hard that I noticed the room was growing dark while I was gasping for air. He finally let go after I blacked out for a couple of seconds and I fell to the ground. I still don't understand how I never had internal bleeding or more than the welt he left below my eye.

    After he left for work and I was waiting to walk to my bus stop for school, my nanny and I were sitting in the kitchen talking. She noticed I was continuously looking down and wouldn't make eye contact with her. She eventually got me to look up at her into her eyes. She saw the pain behind my eyes along with part of my face swollen. She asked me multiple questions that I couldn't answer. I sat there quietly trying to hold back the tears. That's when she put everything together and learned what he was doing.

As livid as she was; she immediately wanted to pick up the phone and call the cops as any adult would do, but I begged and pleaded for her to wait until there was hardcore evidence because I could not risk Kent getting out of jail for the sake of my life. I had to be strategic on revealing him because I only had one chance and I couldn't risk him getting out of prison to hunt me down and kill me. I didn't know at the time that I was sent an angel to help me. My nanny and I established a code word for the next time he had sex with me and then we would move forward to get the cops involved.

I had been cheated for seven years of my childhood. I couldn't even have a television in my room and enjoy it because I would be forced to watch porn at night whenever Kent would sneak into my room to have sex with me. That emptiness had been filled with resentment, anger, self-hatred, guilt, and numbness.

Hunting season was a big deal for Kent while we were living in Colorado. My family decided to plan and host an annual meat party. It was the night before the party and my mom was in a frantic hurry because she still needed to go to a couple of stores and get the rest of the supplies for the big event. She decided to take my three younger siblings with her. I begged to go with her since she was taking all the other kids, but Kent convinced her that he needed my help getting the house prepared for the following day. So, it was just Kent and I alone in that toxic house. Another sex opportunity was presented to him.

    I was downstairs cleaning and he had disappeared upstairs. Shortly after I heard him call my name to come upstairs, I already knew what was about to happen. So of course, I drug my feet and took as much time as possible in hopes mom would be back before he could take advantage of my body. As I dreadfully made it to the top of the stairs, I was so scared to look in my parent's bedroom. I turned my head to the left and made instant eye contact with Kent as he was sitting in his favorite blue lawn chair by the bed in their bedroom; naked and stroking his penis with a pornographic film playing behind him. He told me to come in the room, but my feet wouldn't move, and I hesitated. He noticed I wasn't moving, and he became more aggressive and threatened to beat me. When I entered the room, he made me kneel to my knees and give him oral sex. Shortly after he proceeded to have intercourse with me.

It was bittersweet that he left his sperm lingering inside of me. As he slipped away into the backyard to enjoy his blunt, I rushed to the phone to call our nanny and gave her the code word. While I was on the phone with my nanny, she had her mom call the cops and hung up with me to call SVU. I was so scared I didn't want to hang up the phone with her because I had no idea what was about to happen and felt so alone.

I Could Be Worse

The cops slowly crept up to our house in their cars, ironically at the same time my mom pulled into our driveway. The two officers approached her as she was unloading the bags from the car. They asked to speak with her about a complaint they received at our address and asked to come inside. They were able to separate my parents from me. They had them seated in the television room in the front of the house, while they brought me into the kitchen near the back of the house. They started asking me questions about to try to learn the nature of the call. Was something was going on at the house? Was I in danger? As streams of tears ran out of my eyes, I looked at them and verbally told them the opposite of what was going on because I knew Kent was listening to us from the other room. As I was verbally answering the questions incorrectly, I was signaling with my head the correct answers at the same time. They asked me to step outside where it was more private so I could safely talk to them.

    On the way out the door I ran upstairs to my room to grab my coat and gloves. Somehow Kent managed to make his way up the stairs to greet me as I was about to come back down. He instantly gripped my arm as hard as he could, he gave me this evil cold-hearted look and with a enforcement in his voice he threatened me to not say a word to those cops about him and I, or else he would kill me. Running down the stairs with nothing but fear in my body, my heart was pounding out of my chest and I knew that this was my only chance to get out. I knew I was about to risk my short-lived life by telling the truth.

I followed the two police officers out the front door into the frigged cold. As I was standing there in between the two of them I felt my hands and toes turning numb, they both looked at me attentively waiting for me to tell them what they came to hear. Little did I know the house was surrounded with cops waiting to be given the signal to approach the house. I was finally in a safe zone and Kent couldn't hear me with the brick walls keeping us separated. I hesitated telling them what happened and had to find the courage to tell. Standing in that moment, I told myself everything will be okay, this was my only chance and this time I had hardcore DNA that he couldn't talk his way out of.

    With a jolt of courage, I told them what had happened that night and what Kent had been doing to me.

They both looked at each other in shock of what they just heard. They told me that I was going to be escorted off the premises because of the information I had disclosed. I started panicking and begged them to handcuff me while escorting me to the car to make it look like I was in trouble so Kent wouldn't suspect anything. They declined my request and told me that I was the victim and did nothing wrong.

After I was escorted to the back of the police car the officers called their backups to go ahead and approach the house. I swear it was like S.W.A.T coming to raid the house. Another episode of *Law and Order: SVU* moment to moment. I dismissed the hard and cold seat because of all the action going on outside the car. Once SVU arrived at the scene I was escorted to her car.

When I looked out the car window, I saw nothing but chaos going in and out of my house. The officers had arrested Kent and isolated him from my mom and siblings. They were hauling out the illegal guns and searching the house for drugs. An officer had escorted my mom outside and told her the one secret I was terrified for her to know. She dropped to her knees sobbing. I wanted to jump out of the car and run to her so I could hug her tight. I wanted to tell her that everything was going to be okay and that I was okay. But I couldn't because I was constrained to the car. That memory of my mom's reaction when the police told her the real reason they were called and why they were there, will forever be stained in my brain. The police officer we were waiting on to escort the SVU advocate and myself to the hospital had finally showed up.

When I got taken back to the exam room, it was a very frightening experience. There was a room full of strangers pulling and probing me. The exam had happened so fast and everyone was very meticulous. It put me at ease when they constantly let me know what they were doing each step of the way. The detective assigned to the case had been contacted and was notified to come to the hospital to ask me questions so he could start his investigation. I was so scared to face my mother because I didn't know what she was going to say, if she was going to believe me, or blame me for breaking up the family. So many thoughts ran through my head.

After the doctors were done with the rape kit, they put me in a small private room where the detective had been waiting there to greet me. That was when I was notified that my mom was on the way. I really didn't want her to come though I wanted my dad. I was so scared to face her; all I could think about was how much she probably hated me for ruining her life. The more I thought about it the more my hands became sweaty and my anxiety shot out the roof. I couldn't stop crying because of the unknown and what was about to.

All these years my brain has trained itself to believe I am not good enough. I am not good enough to be a friend, to be a daughter, to be loved, to be a mother, I'm not good enough for myself. And any situation that goes wrong that involves me (even when I had no control of it) it validates my thought of why I am not good enough. I know it may be silly to some, but being held hostage in your own body and constantly being told, "you will never be anything, nobody loves you, you are a failure and a screw up" by the one person who replaced my biological father. Eventually those words became believable and were embedded in me.

2.

Take The Stand

February 15, 2011

"Dear diary,
No Choir Boy. I have noticed that this book has had an emotional effect on me. There is so much connection made between those criminals and me. When reading this novel, it reminds me of Kent. Is he experiencing what those criminals are experiencing, maybe worse? This book triggers a confusing emotion. I hate the government and the system. How can you put a kid on death row for an accidental murder, but if a rapist rapes a little girl for seven years consecutively, he is still given the chance to walk free? Any person who has the audacity to commit such a heinous crime shouldn't be given a second chance to live. The innocence he stole from that little girl won't be returned to her. Those years of being a child, he stole from her. She doesn't get another chance; she doesn't get those years lost or her innocence.

When I look back, I used to be a prisoner. The way those convicts described their newfound life in prison was exactly how I felt except I wasn't locked behind metal bars, I was locked up in my own body."

-Larissa Clark

What's next… they know now. I'm scared. I hope I don't get in trouble for telling. Is Kent going to find me and kill me? Does my mom believe me? Do the police believe me? I'm an embarrassment. I ruined my family's life and now they hate me. It was all my fault that all this happened to me. I am so stupid for saying anything, now my siblings are going to grow up without a dad. What was I thinking, I should've kept my mouth shut?

The years I have waited for the right opportunity to tell my kept secret. I was in a position where Kent wouldn't be given the chance to talk his way to freedom, so he could hunt me down and kill me for telling what he had been doing to me. It was all a reality now, those many nights I laid in bed daydreaming of how this scenario would go, is now a reality. The time had come for me to be strong and send him to prison for everything that he had done to me all those years.

After the detective was done getting a statement from me at the hospital and my mom got there we were able to leave, fortunately we weren't able to go home because our house was taped off due to the investigation, so we ended up having to stay with my mom's friend for a few days. Within a matter of days after leaving the hospital I had to go to the police station to get photos taken of the bruises and marks that were left on my body from Kent, they were using this as evidence for the trial. Then we had to go to the advocacy center to give a detailed testimony about my abuse. Where it happened, how it happened, and when it happened. The biggest question still unanswered today is "why did it happen?"

My mom was heartbroken because of what happened to me, but she was my rock. She made sure I got where I needed to go and that I got all the services I needed to be able to start the healing process. My dad drove up to Denver a couple of times to help with my appointments and support my mom through these traumatic events. Not once did she ever second guess if I was telling the truth or not. She believed me from the start, which was my biggest fear in telling her. I thought she was going to dismiss the abuse and continue staying with my stepdad because she loved him, was in denial, tell me I'm lying he would never do something like that because he is a good man and father, or ask, "what did you do for him to do that to you?". I know that my childhood was stripped from me, which as a mom today I believe it's my responsibility that my daughter doesn't ever have to endure a life like that. I will always believe what my child tells me no matter who it may involve and do my due diligence as her mother to protect her.

  I couldn't have done it alone! It would not have been possible for me to go through the whole process from being at the hospital doing a rape kit by myself to attending the court sentencing alone. I am so grateful for the Denver police, investigator, and defense attorney that were assigned to my case, they worked so hard and carefully on my behalf.

I am very appreciative and thankful for the family members who came from out of state and the friends that were in state to help support my mom and I throughout the prosecution, the high school faculty for being flexible knowing that I was missing a lot of school because of court hearings and appointments, and the therapist I was working with at the time for mentally prepping me for the day I got to take the stand in the court room.

The court hearings began when I reached high school. Unfortunately, the jury trial date kept getting pushed until finally my Sophomore year. They finally set the date for the fall of 2008. It was finally time to tell my story and let my voice be heard after seven and a half dreadful years. Kent couldn't run from me anymore and my plan was to stare him in his eye while I was on stand, so he knew I wasn't scared of him anymore.

After many therapy sessions of preparation for the big day and countless meetings with the defense attorney and investigator, the long-awaited day had finally arrived. During those two weeks, it included a variety of witnesses affiliated with Kent both professional and personal, a large quantity of objects that were used as evidence, the test results from the rape kit, my mom's and dad's testimony and then there was me. I got to skip school the day I testified because it was going to be an all-day event. My mom, dad, and I drove to the courthouse when the day had come for us to take the stand and testify. My parents were called to the stand before I was, but I had to wait in the waiting room with my therapist while they were being questioned in the courtroom.

My anxiety was through the roof, my knee wouldn't stop bouncing and it was so hard for me to sit still. There were a thousand thoughts running through my head and the anticipation was building up. I didn't know if I could follow through with this. I was second guessing my decision for moving forward to a jury trial, maybe it would've been safer to take the plea bargain, so I didn't have to sit there and see him while I was telling my story. What if he finds a way to get out and hunts me down so he can kill me, what if he hires someone to kill me, I don't want anyone feeling sorry for me. What if the jury doesn't believe me, what if he walks away free because they find him not guilty…?

That's when my therapist stepped in and we talked it through. She reminded me why I was in that room sitting in that chair. My long awaited seven years of torture had ended and that was the day where I got to tell my story and put him away forever so he couldn't hurt my siblings or anyone else ever again. She reminded me that I am strong and that he can't hurt me because he will be shackled to the desk and can't get up.

Take The Stand

The defense attorney walked into the room, gave me the look and told me it was time. I didn't know what to expect even though she had prepped me what felt like a thousand times, but I still didn't know what I was about to walk into. I followed her and this other gentleman down the hall in the direction of the room where the trial was being held. I was reminded before I went in the room that I can do it, this is the moment I had been waiting for. I was called to the stand and I swore under oath before I sat down. It was the most gut-wrenching moment I have ever felt. So many people looking at me, so many unfamiliar faces, and there he was. Kent was sitting in front of me – but slightly to the right – with his jail suit on.

Take The Stand

The questioning process began from both sides of the benches. I had to tell so many gruesome details and point to all the objects that he ever used on me, even the sex toys he used on me and had to describe everything he did and made me do. While I was on stand terrified, I could see in my peripheral vision that majority of jurors had flooded eyes and tears streaming down their faces with tissues in their hands and the rest of them spent their time glaring at Kent with disgust from across the room. The whole time I testified I stared at him, I wanted him to know that I wasn't scared of him anymore and that EVERYONE in that room was going to know what he had done to me and I was going to tell it proud. But he never gave me that satisfaction, he never once looked me in the eye. He looked down the whole time I was on stand testifying.

After stepping down from the stand I was applauded for how well I did, how strong I stayed on the stand, and I didn't let the public defender bully me into saying anything that wasn't true. How everyone viewed me I didn't view myself that way. It still felt so surreal to me and it didn't seem like a big deal, in my mind I knew that's just what needed to be done.

On February 4, 2009 Kent was sentenced to life without parole in prison for being found guilty on all 28 charges from my one case. The crimes he committed on me were so heinous that if he were to be released from prison, he would've been tried in two other states for committing those same crimes on me.

As I watched Kent shuffle out the doors, I knew that chapter in my life had finally ended and I would never have to see him again, or fear for my life again. A huge sigh of relief came over my body from the results I just heard. No one should ever have to go through what I went through, nor should anyone go through anything close to it. To live a life full of anger, pain, and fearfulness knowing their perpetrator never was held accountable for the crime they– how do we change that?

I acknowledge that my case was a victory case and not a lot of victims get the justice they deserve. I was given the opportunity to hold my perpetrator accountable, but just because he was, it will never compensate for the amount of emotional, physical, and verbal restraint Kent put on me for all of those years.

After we were dismissed from the sentencing hearing, my mom pulled me aside to introduce me to a very nice lady – who was one of the jurors that was sitting on the jury panel during my trial. She said she came to the sentence hearing because she wanted to meet me and was there on behalf of all the other jurors. She told me how strong I was to go through everything that I did, but still be able to testify against him. She told me how happy she was for me and that she had a daughter younger than me and I helped her open her eyes as a mother, and that she will walk away from being a witness to my experience a different woman. In that moment I realized that this was the beginning of a journey where God gave me the ability to help others in many ways naturally and unknowingly.

Seven and a half years of my childhood were stripped from me and I was at a disadvantage mentally because it affected my developmental growth emotionally. I had to relearn how to function in society all over again, I had to relearn how to be able to feel feelings – how to control and understand them. My abuse even caused physical damage; till this very day I struggle orgasming without any clitoral stimulation. I have to mentally go into a deep state of mind in order to relax during intercourse so I'm able to stay present and not disassociate. Those are huge hurdles I had to overcome and still am today as an adult.

3.

The Dark Road Alone

June 19, 2013

"Dear diary,
my mind can only wonder so far. I frustrate myself and others frustrate me. I just want to run somewhere and never come back. Forget everything that was left behind and start a new life. I know I'm not perfect and I make a lot of mistakes and a lot of times I'm to prideful to admit that. I feel like I'm going crazy. I feel lost like there is no one who I can actually trust and release my secrets buried in the box. This world is full of evil, hatred, and deceitfulness. I really need to go back to counseling; I feel the world getting heavier and heavier and God has blessed me with only so much strength."

-Larissa Clark

I've always been known to be innovative in order to create ways to make money. My first year having my own place in Houston and wasn't returning to school for that upcoming semester, so I applied and got hired onto Hooters as a waitress. A lot of young girls' dream! It was a lot of fun and I made a ton of money! Something I could get used to. Besides, I was used to using my looks and body figure for getting what I wanted when I wanted it. During that time, I got a second job to bring in some extra money so I could make sure all the bills could get paid. The owner of an escorting company based in Denver offered me an enticing opportunity that I didn't make sense to decline. I needed extra cash and from the stories and reviews. It was good money.

This was a very professional and very legal opportunity, so I felt at ease with what I was doing, but still had no idea what I was getting myself into. Meeting my first client was not at all what I expected. I learned very quickly that I had to be smart about my time and no matter what always stay in a public place. It was a very scandalous industry and even though the company took precautions of your safety they could only do so much being so far away. I didn't last long working for that company after my last uncomfortable experience.

Shortly after I left both places, I met a nice man through a mutual friend, which at the time I didn't know was an up-and-coming pimp. Little did I know I was about to be to in a different line of work that involved a lot of men who were customers and women that couldn't walk away because of the fast money. I was in a bind for money and desperate to make sure my bills got paid. My first club I worked at was a whole in the wall, but I still managed to make decent money. After being there for a short period of time, I got hired at a more upscale club where all the girls were well taken care of. As time passed on, I quickly learned that this industry is the devil's playground – and I was in the center of it. I'm grateful that location didn't require the girls to be nude. So essentially, I felt like I was back at Hooters again.

I had to be smart about the way I worked, because it was very fast-paced and a very competitive industry – especially if you weren't volunteering your goodies. While girls were stumbling everywhere drunk and, in the back, doing drugs to escape their reality, my natural high was creating this person who men worshipped and idolized. It got to the point where I finally mastered disassociation and my persona. Every time I stepped foot into that building and put the wig on, I was my alter-ego and I loved it. I got to create the person that I wanted to be, who wasn't damaged and didn't have a horrible traumatic background.

    A world where I could escape and create whatever story I wanted and be there for miserable married men who were just looking for a pretty face to talk to. It was a natural high being desired by so many men and them not being able to have me. It was all about control, that one thing that I've never been given the chance to experience all of my life.

Even though I didn't turn to drugs and excessive alcohol like a lot of girls did in order to get through the day, my poison of choice was disassociation and living out my alter ego. But it was because it felt *good* internally, not because I had a guilty conscience, nor did I have a bad home life. I got comfortable with the money I was making, my relationships I had established, and the alter-ego I had created. Life was nothing but a party and I loved going to work every day, but I truly believe God thought more of me and had a different plan.

I have always had a positive opinion about police officers because growing up I was taught they work to keep me safe, and they proved it when they helped protect me from the person that I feared the most in the world. My opinion broadened because of the situation that occurred, and till this day that occurrence still shocks me that that even took place. I felt like I had the worst luck and always happen to be in the wrong place at the wrong time, but I have a suspicion that usually when bizarre situations occur it's because I am not living my life the way I am supposed to be.

    I just remember when I was driving, I turned the corner to go down the street, I noticed police cars were coming from all directions, but didn't realize they were coming for me and forcefully pulled me over. As I was pulling off the street all I could think about was why am I getting pulled over, did I have a taillight out, or did I not turn on my signal. When they got out the car and came to my window, they asked to search my car then started asking me a lot of abnormal questions.

I was so embarrassed to let them search my car because I had my dance bag in my trunk, and I didn't want them going through it let alone come up with assumptions. By this point I still had no idea what was going on or why I got pulled over. As they were searching my car, I started conversing with the lead sergeant of the narcotic department and come to find out I happened to be sitting idle in my car at the wrong place at the wrong time. I had NEVER had any type of negative encounters with the police and that situation left me feeling concerned.

    I feel it was God giving me a sign about the way I was living my life at that time and to get out of the dancing industry, so I didn't have to continue to lie to everyone about what I was doing and do more for myself career wise.

After that situation there were a series of events that started happening towards the end of my dancing career that made me transition out of that industry within a year and a half, which was great timing because I saw a huge decrease in my income due to all the changes.

I did take something away when I left the dancing industry: I took away knowing how to be a master of disassociation, how to be comfortable and embrace my bare skin, and how to be proficient in sales. Being in a sensual environment for so long sparked a flame in me after I had left the industry. I gained curiosity in my sexuality and found myself wanting to explore and experiment. I found myself looking at women in a different way, wanting to be in a more mature environment and witnessing things in real life you would see on pornography films, and I loved every moment of it, it was my new high.

Sex is a curse for me, I always blamed myself and thought something was wrong with me for always being sexually curious before my abuse even occurred. During my abuse I convinced myself that I deserved what happened to me because of my natural curiosity of sex. I believed that if I never had asked Kent what sex was behind closed doors in confidence then I would have never opened the flood gates to living the nightmare I endured. I don't know if what I went through was good or bad when it comes to my sexuality. I find myself very aware of my body and am very sensual. I am open minded and like to take things to the next level – past *Fifty Shades of Grey* level. It took a *long* time to gain control of my sexuality, which wasn't my proudest period of life. There was a period where I was destructive and careless, and with drunken nights came drunken sex. It was my next level of disassociation, and when you added drugs into the mix I was on top of the world.

During that gap that I wasn't going to therapy or getting mental help, I was getting assistance elsewhere. More than anything reckless, constant sex was my drug of choice. It felt great in the moment and I was always the dominating person and in control. After having so much of the same level of sex, I grew bored and I needed to take things to the next level of excitement. The more I stayed away from therapy and other positive factors in my life, the more sex became an addiction that I couldn't get enough of. I didn't want to pursue those partners for relationships beyond sex. I would use them then dump them.

I'm fortunate that that time period lasted for only a few years, once I sought out therapy again and started attending sessions. I started understanding what the addiction meant, where it stemmed from, and how to process the desire.

Chapter 4: I'm Doing Great, Thanks for Asking

February 7, 2019

"Dear diary,
 I had EMDR today and it was more of a mental struggle for me. I was able to unblock the sex acts that my stepdad did to me. I am so livid because I finally understand that he took something away from me. And it shows till this very day. I am angry that I can't connect with Sam on the level I want because of his behavior, what he says to me, and how he treats me. It reminds me of my stepdad. I feel my mind starting to shift away from all the bad habits I've always done to help me cope. Drink, sex, being destructive, etc. So, what now? What is God trying to show me? How I view people. I feel more scared than ever to get close to people because I'm in a vulnerable state in my life and can't afford getting hurt because that's not what life is about. I'm on a journey I can't explain. I'm not alone when I don't isolate myself. People love me and care I just have to let the right ones in and take the wrong ones out."

-Larissa Clark

I struggled a lot understanding my PTSD and how to work through episodes. The first two years in high school were miserable because I was always going to counseling, prepping for court, overcoming triggers and flashbacks. That's when I got introduced to ecstasy and weed brownies and mild pills. I thank the Lord that I do not have an addictive personality, especially that time in my life. I was acting out – not because I wanted to be defiant and disobedient, but because I couldn't control what was going on the inside and I had to find a release or something to put that energy into. This was before I learned about healthy coping, I was in pre self-destruct mode. My senior year of high school I finally found my kryptonite. Her name could be any name as long as she was in a bottle and it was liquid! I found my aid to help me escape from within. In college it got worse. I was more interested in drinking than having boyfriends. I also thank God that I didn't go off the deep end and still managed to attend college classes, the ones I went to anyway and I went to them very sober.

Suffering from PTSD isn't the proudest thing I like to converse about. PTSD is a *real thing*. It's amazing to see and hear all the negative opinions from society on their outlook of individuals seeking professional help with their mental state of mind. A lot of people like to smirk at it and not take it seriously. We don't truly know how it works in a person because everyone who has experienced a traumatic event that caused the PTSD lives with it differently, so who are we to press judgement. I have always felt like an outsider because of this heavy, dark, painful thing I carry around with me on my back every day. So as long as I keep a smile on my face and act like everything is okay, I will fit in and I'll be classified as normal, but little did everyone know that I was struggling to wake up and just breathe let alone live every day. At this point in my life I have mastered the facade of everything is okay. It's easier to pretend to be happy then it is explaining what's wrong with me to someone who really doesn't care because they have their own problems in their life.

When my long-term abuse was discovered, there were a variety of doctors that I had to see for different reasons. When I went to see a psychiatrist, she diagnosed me with PTSD. She prescribed me medication for the insomnia and medication for my anxiety and depression.

Now I am a very stubborn person as you may get to figure that out throughout the book. When my mom got the medications, I told her to keep it. I didn't want to take it for several reasons:

1. Because I didn't want to get tempted to take one to many sleeping pills and not wake up.

2. I didn't know what my reaction would be to the anxiety/depression and I couldn't allow myself to venture into the unknown because I was a control freak.

3. I wanted to fight this disorder by using holistic techniques, whatever that looked like. I wanted to gain control over my PTSD, thoughts, spiraling feelings, anger, pain, triggers and flashbacks holistically. I didn't want to

be going through this healing process as a cold zombie. So, I never went back to see a psychiatrist again until the beginning of 2019.

I was struggling with severe insomnia, depression, and anxiety. My anxiety would get so bad that I would start to hyperventilate and couldn't breathe while the walls in the room were closing in. It turned into a flashback from the past, where I felt like I was having a panic attack while I was in class. I would often have to leave the room because they would be so severe that I was gasping for air and would be sent to the in-school counselor in order to learn how to find grounding through these panic attacks.

I was diagnosed by my psychologist and psychiatrist as a Manic-Depressive with severe anxiety. I wasn't eating or sleeping and when I was sleeping my dreams were so vivid and intense that they wouldn't allow me to stay asleep. My psychiatrist prescribed me Trazadone to help with my sleep and another medication that's most recommended for depression/anxiety. This was my first time ever considering taking this medication and I was terrified because once again I didn't know how I was going to react. I asked her a lot of questions and my main question was " if this drug isn't used to supplement a chemical that I could be lacking to make me feel this way and it's pretty much a Band-Aid for my problems and feelings, why take it?" I wanted a more holistic approach where I could heal the root of the issue, not just mitigate the symptoms. Her response was: It's only temporary to help get you through what you are going through then when your numbers go down, we will ween you off the medication. I don't have anything against medication I just made a promise to myself and I wasn't going to break that promise just for a temporary Band-Aid. I proceeded to research other holistic options, I did get my sleeping medication which I only took when my anxiety was really high before I went to bed, which was practically every night. They even upped my dosage after taking it for a couple of months because it wasn't strong enough. Well today, I've managed to decrease the days I take it and am at the point where I only take it once in a Blue Moon.

I've been seeing psychologists on and off for 12 years now. It's sad looking back of how much time I wasted because I never took it seriously and didn't do the work until these past couple of years I will say that these past 2 years of therapy have saved my life and I am beginning to gain freedom from my own chains. My current therapist and I started a different form of therapy called Eye Movement Desensitization and Reprocessing, also known as EMDR. Therapists have been starting to use this method on patients with all forms of PTSD. I have a severe form of PTSD due to the amount of trauma I suffered for so many of my childhood and adolescent years.

According to EMDR Institute, Inc. "Eye Movement Desensitization and Reprocessing (EMDR) is a psychotherapy treatment that was originally designed to alleviate the distress associated with traumatic memories. EMDR is the newer form of therapy structured to help people heal from traumatic or detrimental life experiences. When going through this type of treatment you are instructed to focus on a traumatic event that occurred in your life and must zone in to relive that memory. As you are in the zone, the therapist will then use different forms of techniques to keep your mind concentrated on that specific event, which will make your mind channel into what happened during that time. EMDR is programmed to be a 13-week session or less depending on the trauma that is being worked on, but since my trauma is so complex and occurred for so many years I am expected to be doing EMDR for a matter of years, instead of months.

It's so interesting to see how everything is connected unconsciously and I would've never learned that if I hadn't started the EMDR program. It's such an amazing form of therapy. I have learned so much about myself, I have been managing to close the doors that have been lingering open and addressing issues that have been buried deep within. The downfall is my brain protects itself from itself, so my disassociation increased along with my urge to self-medicate, but I have been slowly noticing myself shifting in a different direction. The way I speak, and the way I think! Even the people that are actively involved in my life are noticing a difference as well.

The goal during our EMDR sessions is to focus on the memories that cause present disturbance to help future actions and to depart with emotions and understanding that will guide to healthy behaviors and interactions. During our weekly session we focus on the negative cognition that my brain thinks and pick a memory it is attached to. The goal is to turn that negative thought into a positive and process that memory. Once I don't have any butterfly sensations throughout my body when focusing on that particular memory then I have come to peace with that negative cognition. Now when I say feeling in my body, that is how the psychologist knows if that issue has been solved otherwise, I will have feelings in any part of the body letting her know that is where I am carrying that issue.

This form of therapy is miraculous and since I started EMDR and I stay consistent with my weekly sessions I notice that my craving to drink alcohol all the time decreased, my desire to have emotionless sex so I can disassociate has started to decrease. I am becoming more in control over my anxiety and gaining self-awareness when I feel my depression or anxiety creeping in. I am learning how to master emotional grounding and stay present when doing so and I also have processed and resolved the smaller issues that have been manifesting. The biggest one is I worry less and have learned to resort to healthy coping instead of being destructive!

Currently in EMDR we are working on overcoming the negative thought that, "I'm not good enough". I know that may sound easily adjustable, but it isn't as easy for me as you would think it to be. Years of being told this time and time again that thought has been stained in my brain and I am consistently reminded why I am not good with a variety of situations and events. I can I train myself to believe that I am good enough when these life events prove otherwise.

For example, I was hopefully getting this position I was really excited to be a part of; however, I got the same generic email saying they selected another candidate, but I was great. It's the worst feeling hearing someone say I'm not fit enough to be a part of their organization, even though I'm qualified and fit the criteria. I have been struggling with being told no by so many companies since October of 2018. I have no issue getting an interview or being a top candidate, but I always win the *you almost got the position* award. It is so discouraging, why even try when no matter how hard I try or how much I go above and beyond to display my passion I'm still not good enough. That's why I struggle till this very day of "what is my purpose?" I realize it may not be the plan that I want it to be, but God has a different plan and I still don't have a clue what it is.

How do I overcome not being good enough? The evidence shows no matter where I go or what I do, I'm never good enough. That is where EMDR comes handy because eventually we find the root memory that is attached to this negative cognition then it transforms into, "I am good enough" once I thoroughly process the memory that I have been burrowing. That is one of four negative cognitions my brain tells itself and believes that we know of so far "I am not good enough", "I am not lovable," "I cannot protect myself," and "I can't trust anyone".

Sadly, I recently closed the chapter with my current therapist and am in the process to move forward with a more experienced therapist that has specialized in EMDR for many years. It was extremely sad and hard for me to end that relationship with my therapist because she has helped me in extreme ways and took genuine interest in me that I haven't had in my life for a long time. She has been the only person that was consistent in my life throughout the two years of having sessions with her. She saved me from jumping of the ledge on many occasions and helped guide me to view things in a different perspective.

She is the reason why my wall started crumbling down, any other therapist I had in the past my wall was always up and I would always put on a front to portray that everything was okay in my life, but with her she would always see right past it. I could never thank her enough for being such an influence too me in my life and giving me the nudge I needed when needed. Because I struggle with abandonment issues, it was so painful to say farewell to her because she was someone that I opened myself up to and was able to be vulnerable, but then she vanished out of my life unexpectedly. It just feels like another death, but I know it's because god knows I am ready to take the next step in EMDR and the next step she couldn't help me with because that is beyond her practice and training.

    I can make peace with our relationship because she helped me realize that I don't know how to be loved, or what being loved really looks like in an intimate relationship. I stay strong and am there for everyone, but I'm not there for myself. My therapist says I am in a cleansing phase in my life and starting to realize and follow through on what makes Larissa happy, which I haven't done in a very, very long time Even though she says I have made a tremendous amount of progress and is proud of me, I still feel like a underachiever and I feel that I am unlovable.

5.

Dear God, Are You There?

March 14, 2011

"Dear diary,
I don't deal with my emotions. I block them out and I block whoever triggers my emotions out to. It's painful, in order for me to be happy I need to deal with the sadness and anger that is built in me. It eats me up every day, being trapped as a prisoner in my own body. How, how do I deal with these harsh emotions without running away, I can't that's who I am, what I am. Running away is what I'm good at, that's all I know. I squirm with the thought of dealing with my emotions and it affects letting people in. Will I ever have a healthy relationship and trust to the fullest? That to me is unknown because in the back of my mind I will always have my guard up."

-Larissa Clark

Going through my EMDR journey has caused me to be in a healthier and more balanced state – both physically and mentally. It has enhanced my walk with God and allowed me to embrace positive change in my life and my spirit because I am now getting fed through a mental health portal and spiritual portal. This allows me to pursue God in a healthier way, as opposed to my previous coping mechanisms of destruction and defiance. A clearer mind has led me to clearer answers.

I didn't have strong faith until I was 22. I know there is this huge argument about whether there is or isn't a "God" – I think it really comes down to *'to each their own'*. Everyone has a right to believe what they want. I don't claim religion – instead, I claim a spiritual relationship with the higher power. In my 20's, during an all-time low, I finally surrendered.

In the past I have always been tense when it came to faith and religion, especially with the viewpoint I had because of my abuse. It is such a touchy subject when having a conversation involving rape and faith at the same time. I have interacted with individuals on the whole spectrum believing God is not real and there is no higher power all the way to believing that if you have one sip of alcohol then you're going to hell. So, I have always kept my mouth shut about my many kept dark secrets because I didn't want to be judged and be condemned by other people.

Growing up we always hopped from church to church, my family did however find a couple of good churches along the way. I didn't really believe in God especially once my abuse started. I always thought why this so-called God would make me this innocent little girl go through something horrible for so long. It led me to become an atheist and believing in luck instead of having faith.

Throughout that time, I continuously asked myself, how could there be a God if he let Kent rape me of my innocence for all those years? It always made me wonder what did I do to deserve this? How can I go to church every Sunday to hear the word and the pastor preach about God being a good God and will protect you? When in the end the day I felt that all those things never applied to me. I believe that I was angry with God for so many years because it was so hard for me to process and accept that good people go through horrible experiences for a reason. There were many days and nights that I remember my stepfather being on top of me and as I laid there helpless with my eyes tightly shut, all I could think to myself was how is there a God because if there was a God he would not let a grown man have sex with a twelve-year-old.

It took so long for me to not be angry anymore and truly embrace that Higher Power. It wasn't until I was 20 when I finally surrendered because my life had hit rock bottom to the point where I had no home and was living in the backyard in a mutual friend's trailer. Both of my parents weren't talking to me at the time for different reasons, I was completely lost in my life, and the little guidance I had was from horrible influences. All I had left with me was my clothes in a couple of bins and my dog who got me through those suicidal moments. After being put in that situation that's when I surrendered, and I said ok, God, what do you want for me? Please show me the way. It's been a rough journey and God has continuously been testing me since 2011 up to now.

I must say that the year of 2019 was one of my most challenging and trying years I've ever had. I was faced with so many triggering emotions that forced me to learn how to process past issues and feelings that I've buried and disassociated from over the years. This was the year where God opened new doors and closed doors unexplainably that have left me in nothing but a puddle of tears. This year I went through heartbreak, I went through losing myself and not knowing my purpose in life, and I went through not knowing who I am as a person, but still had to wake up every day to be a functioning mother for my daughter. This was the year I had more suicidal thoughts than I had all the seven years that I was molested by my stepfather.

By the grace of God every challenge I faced and overcame brought me closer to him. Every day when I was struggling, I dropped to my knees and I prayed "please just give me the guidance please just give me the strength, close the wrong doors and open the right doors. For I know that anything that I go through I will survive because you will not put me through anything I cannot handle".

In 2017, getting baptized became heavy on my conscious and I wanted to do before my daughter was born.

I wanted to start my life on a clean slate and live my life in a more meaningful, less defiant way. I knew that I hadn't been living my life right all these years and I wanted to make it right with god, but he had a different plan. I assume that moment in time wasn't right timing for me to get baptized maybe because God wasn't ready for me to take the next step because he was still working on me.

On August 18th, 2019 I finally followed through on my commitment I made to myself and took the biggest step of my life. I got baptized. After I got baptized, I've noticed I haven't been that same person since and he continuously works through me in ways that I could never explain how nor even know why. It's crazy how everything unexplainably falls into place and the events that occur in the order they do. As each day goes by, I feel myself shifting and molding into the person that I am supposed to become and touch individuals' lives in ways I never knew were possible.

Faith has become such a strong priority in my life. The same day I got baptized was the same day that my daughter's father and I decided to take our relationship to court and establish child support as well as joint custody. And till this day I wonder if it was the devil trying to tear me down or if it was God relieving me of this kept secret and frustration that I had been holding in for months.

In the back of my mind I always have to remember to reconcile with God, so I am able to reconcile with others and it all starts with forgiving myself. I am my worst critic, which I'm probably not the only person that does that. Before I got baptized and really sought out spiritual growth within myself, I had so much animosity, worry, sorrow, low self-esteem, and consistent anxiety that would linger. And in result it would manifest into anger, hatred, and envy. I was so conflicted with in myself that it was affecting the relationships I had surrounding me.

If I had never taken that step into EMDR and gotten this far in the process, I believe I wouldn't have become as self-aware and recognize those feelings and understanding as to why I am feeling the way I do, but instead I would be in the same head space and have the same thought process as I always have.

It all started with forgiveness.

Forgiving myself. I wasn't always the nicest person to myself and am still learning how to fall in love with who I am more, recognize the accomplishments I've made this far even though I'm not where I want to be today, forgiving myself for all the mistakes I've made and the people that I have hurt throughout my life, knowing that what Kent did to me wasn't my fault, and I may not be everyone's cup of tea, but I *am* good enough. Forgiveness isn't necessarily a feeling, it's deliberate and falls in line with obeying god. Forgiveness is a rule in the big book, so why is it so hard.

Forgiving myself has been one of the challenging obstacles I have to overcome in life. As I am learning to forgive myself and those around me, I find more grace and peace in my life and less turmoil and anger. I have recognized that my healthy healing is a combination of EMDR and growing my spiritual relationship. The more I believed in God's will and had faith that he knows what he is doing, he would show me that I wouldn't be put in a situation that I couldn't conquer and overcome.

After I got baptized the way I lived unknowingly changed and the way I reacted to situations changed. I have noticed as my faith grows stronger and I continue to work on mending my brokenness, the more I am challenged with difficult situations that guides me to have a clouded vision, rather than having clear vision.

Sometimes, when I give glory to the things God has saved me from and the blessings he has brought into my life, as detrimental as it is for me people think I am different. It doesn't bother me because I know the truth and so does God. Upon reflection, he has always been watching over me and protecting me in the times where I was most disobedient, he protected me from not getting gang raped by falling asleep at the football house when I was in college, he saved from not getting expelled from school for doing drugs, and so much more. I have always had a conviction, but always ran from it because the anger and hatred I had towards God for all the years of torture I went through. Having God, and accepting that conviction, has transformed me. As I notice God working through my life and transforming me, my eyes have grown more open.

As I'm going through EMDR I have realize, how much pain and hurt I've been carrying through the years and how much destruction I have caused in my life trying to fill a void in order to make the pain disappear just for a moment. I am thankful that I didn't get addicted to drugs, that I didn't become a prostitute or have all kinds of men in and out of my bed every night, that I didn't contract any uncurable diseases, and that I didn't grow hate or resentment in my heart towards my parents or even my perpetrator. That wasn't all therapy's doing, having faith played a big part and a combination other of things.

    It started with acceptance of what happened to me and embracing it, then learning how to love myself and accept who I am, which then came with having better understanding and discipline for my darkest desires.

With the exasperating year I have been having, I am amazed I never got bitter with God, but instead kept crawling back to his feet while weeping in my sorrows and hurt. I haven't shunned my faith and continue to crave growth in my spiritual. After talking to one of my pastors, I came to an understanding that having faith and believing in a God is equivalent to listening and taking advice from a licensed counselor. Not only is it important to have faith because we are spiritual beings, but that is only a portion of the necessities people need to get through this walk we call life. Faith isn't just about focusing on God, but it's about having a strong community and spiritual support. As I am witnessing the growth in my tightknit community, I'm more aware of the type of people I am attracting in my life, who have been beyond supportive and are there when I feel most depressed. I am forever grateful for the genuine people that I have surrounding me in my life because they help give me a push through those hard days and lessen the feeling of feeling alone. I am finally starting to view my life in a different perspective and am now able to pursue my thoughts and transform them into a reality, which in result is becoming a positive and rewarding outcome.

6.

Love Is an Illusion

May 8, 2017

"Dear diary,
I'm bounded. I stray. The resistance.
It hurts when I am around. But why?
I try, I try, but it's not good enough. It will never be good enough. The fire within me awakens.
  VULNERABILITY: How can I? It hurts. They take and walk away leaving me in a black hole to climb out of. I yell for help, but no one hears me.
There's silence.
I'm crazy, I'm lucid, I'm wrong for being who I am. Anger arises leaving broken spirits and puddles of tears. But why? For what reason?
  LOVE: What is love? It is not angry or hurtful. It does not dictate, scorn, tear down, or humiliate. Love is kind, love is caring, love is selfless, love is honesty, and loyalty. Love is understanding, love is non-judgmental, love is SUPPORT. Does this love exist? How does the flower blossom when it isn't being nurtured?
  FORGIVENESS: I forgive you! All of you! All of the disappointments, all of the let downs, all of the broken promises, the manipulation, the bullying, the hurtful things that have been said to tear me down. I've seen you

before in all shapes and sizes. Guess what? YOU WILL NEVER WIN!

<u>STRENGTH:</u> I am powerful and resilient. I can = not be broken. You can bring me down till there is no more floors to fall on. He lays within me, using me, and watching over me. It's not over for me, I'm just beginning, but the end is very near for you.

<u>GAIN:</u> Humility and humbleness, the most beautiful things in life. The perspective and outlook changes. The broken pieces get mended, the heart gets stronger, the smile comes more often, the air gets lighter, the grey clouds disappear, and the vision gets clearer. He grabs my hand with comfort, and I follow down the path behind him!"

-Larissa Clark

A lot of my relationships that I have had throughout my life have been one of my biggest struggles to maintain. And I apologize to the individuals where I disappointed you and let you down as a friend. I apologize for all of the intimate relationships I was in where I wasn't giving the 100% that you wanted me to give. And I apologize to my parents for not living up to your standards and expectations as any parent would want their child to be. As my journey continues in EMDR my mind continues to shift and reflect on how my past life was and the way I could've handled things differently. I recognize those situations that I was in the wrong when at the time I justified why I was right, and you were wrong. I hope that you can forgive me as I have forgiven everyone who has ever wronged me in my life!

I know that I have ongoing daddy issues that haven't been resolved, which is very common these days. I was in disbelief when I learned in EMDR that the triumphs I have been facing throughout my relationships hindered from buried past issues from both of my dad's and were now surfacing. Over the course of time I began to develop abandonment issues and eventually convinced myself that I'm not capable of being loved and am not good enough. And time and time again, I had constantly been reminded of that belief because the individuals who would enter in my life and I entrusted in, vanished with no explanation or reasoning behind it. I was at a disadvantage because I didn't have the tools or knowledge on how to work through those thoughts and issues. In the long run, those unresolved issues were not allowing me to have successful relationships, which hasn't motivated me to maintain healthy relationships throughout the years, especially with the people closest to me.

I have had so many thoughts of ending my life over the years because I felt I wasn't good enough and I wasn't capable of being loved by anyone, not even my own mother or father. I've been a slave trapped in my body since I was seven years old, I've never felt the real feeling of what it feels like to be loved by a man and be treated with love. I'm sure at this point I will have a guard up and it will be so foreign to me because I have never been exposed to it. The only type of impactful relationships with men that have been active in my life brought their own unresolved issues into the relationship, which then effected our relationship and left me with a negative outlook on relationships and hopeless.

After my abuse was discovered the resentment towards both of my parents grew stronger for not knowing what my stepdad did to me. I came to have a better understanding why I had the resentment towards my mother after we processed that feeling through EMDR, but that resentment feeling was a cover up for the true issue, which was feeling like I was a burden on my mom and her life.

I could feel myself developing admiration and envy towards the relationship between my mom and my sister who is eight years younger than me. In my eyes, I felt that my sister was my mom's second chance, I was the abused damaged goods that was unrepairable.

After I graduated high school and I left for college the whole family dynamic changed, and my sister replaced me and became my mom's right-hand girl. My sister was always the people pleaser and strived to not disappoint my mom because she hated getting yelled at. As years passed, they got closer and I grew more distant and continuously acted out, which pushed my mom further away from me. Witnessing my mom's and sister's relationship every time I went home and seeing how much my mom protected my sister compared to the rest of us validated my negative thoughts of being a burden in her life and damaged goods.

I always felt that I couldn't live up to all my sister's accomplishments that made my mom proud. I grew to hate my sister because of how coddled and privileged she was, and yet took advantage of my mom. I know all families have their own problems, but this family has series of problems given the nature of trauma we have all been through, some members are processing and thoroughly working through their issues, while others are acting out and being the victims in all situations.

    It struck anger in me knowing that my sister got that type of treatment even though she wasn't the one who was raped by her dad, yet she was allowed to lash out and mistreat the rest of us because of her own internal issues that she refused to address. It was very frustrating being in a hostile environment whenever my sister was around, especially since that whole dynamic is a major issue that we are working through in my EMDR sessions.

As I continue to process in EMDR, I hope that I will be able to reverse that negative cognition of not being good enough for my mom and come to the realization that it isn't me that is the problem, which will give me more peace than when the feelings originally started to manifest in hopes of influencing the other family members to hold each other accountable in a healthy environment and in a loving way.

I hear and read these stories in books and in the bible about love and healthy relationships, but I've finally acknowledged that my biggest downfall has been believing that I am lovable and that I don't demand how I should be treated in a relationship because I am fearful I will be tossed to the side. All these years I've been convinced that

I'm not good enough and I don't have what it takes to be loved. I am designed for people to just take and take and take from me because I will always give and forgive.

Every intimate relationship started out as a success and hopeful, but became dysfunctional for many reasons, which led us to breaking up and going our separate ways. It showed that I still had unresolved issues internally and was projecting them onto the relationships. As I have been getting deeper into EMDR we are discovering that I have always struggled with trusting people and not being lovable was embedded in me because of my abuse, which started when I was in the most crucial developmental stage of life.

As much as I desired a monogamous relationship and wanting to truly be loved, I didn't know what that looked like because I was never shown it and if I was I didn't know what to do with it, and instead strayed away because I knew it was going to come to an end at some point. All the years of dating my longest relationship was almost a year, until my most recent relationship with Sam. I was faced with a lot of challenges of being honest, committing one hundred percent to every person I was dating at the time, and letting my wall down because I was scared to be vulnerable and give my partner the leeway to get close to me, knowing they were most likely going to take advantage of me and leave me stranded after opening up to them.

My first heart throb was when I was 19, I learned a lot from that relationship, we stayed friends for many years because we didn't live in the same state, but always kept in touch and would visit each other whenever I was in Colorado or he was in Texas. Throughout those years it was strictly platonic, but we had this magnetic attraction towards each other from the time we first met. When he moved closer to Texas, we decided to take things to the next step and be in a committed relationship with one another, eventually he moved back to Texas in the same city I was living in, but it all went downhill from there. We had such an intense relationship that we were always in sync with one another, I quickly learned that we were each other's soul mates; however we didn't always see eye to eye and with a fire and water sign intertwined our passion and love was so strong for each other that it became unbearable, trust was damaged, and resentment and anger was rising. I learned that I love hard, but so hard that it turned toxic.

Even when our relationship ended it was an accidental break up. When we had reconnected after we broke up, we came to an understanding after a long conversation that neither of us broke up with the other, we had just thought we heard both parties ending the relationship. Of course, we ended up laughing about it, but never got back together. I suppose God knew what he was doing. I believe everything happens as it supposed to, but sometimes God steps into situations to handle them for me when I am not capable of following through on my own because at the time it wasn't what I needed, but what I wanted. I don't know where I would have ended up in my life spiritually or even mentally if I was still going down that path with that specific person.

Then came Sam, he was one of the most challenging gut checking relationships I've ever had. I had to learn how to love him and grow to love him. It wasn't natural like my first love, but there was a reason why I chose him to have my beautiful baby with and decided to share my life with him.

Our relationship has never been easy, we have always butted heads since day one because of our egos and stubbornness and it just got more intense the deeper we got into the relationship. I have to say it was one of the most dysfunctional relationships I have ever been in, but you would've never guessed it was going to end up that way.

Throughout the relationship I went face to face with insecurities and anger that I never knew existed until, the chemistry that Sam and I had triggered something within me. Where do my insecurities stem from...why do I feel threatened and feel like I'm not good enough, is it because I'm not tall and slender like the women he's been with throughout his past. Why do I feel not good enough? I don't feel secure. How do I get rid of this feeling? Why does his actions irk me so much? How do I process these feelings and let them go?

My love language is quality time, acts of service, and words of affirmation. I get a thrill doing things for others, but I literally have 1 person in my life that does the same and that's my mom. I don't have many friends and of course that's by choice. My nature has always been on the giving side and loyal to the people I love, but it's unfortunate because that is when I found myself put in predictable positions where I get taken advantage of. With the people I have been attracting through my life and the relationships that I have held they have made feel most alone and skating through life just as another body on this earth. Even in the darkest times that's when I feel most alone, it took for me to leave the state for my friends to reach out and check up on me. I understand that people have their own lives and struggles. Reaching out to my friends and family in time of need has is always such a hard step to take because I always feel that I am inconveniencing people and there are individuals who have validated that feeling over the years, which keeps that thought carrying on.

I am grateful that I went through that experience because I was forced to acknowledge my faults and work on them within myself and of course my therapist was there to assist. I had to learn where my bad habits stemmed from and alter them into healthy habits when it came to coping mechanisms. In moments of high anxiety and panic attacks I would revert to drinking and emotionally shut down. Unfortunately, Sam lacked empathy and wasn't very understanding, nor educated, about PTSD, how it's triggered, and how to help support when under attack. Instead of consoling me through my triggers, he would verbally abuse me and put me down, which would trigger me and take me back to when my stepdad said horrible things to me during my abuse.

Over time, our relationship grew to be full of dishonesty, trust issues, infidelity, which led to unresolved feelings starting to surface. Hidden secrets kept leaking out and we both were at our end's wit, but at this point he was comfortable with his way of life and being able to do whatever he wanted whenever he wanted, while I was scared he would leave and I wasn't in a financially stable place to pay rent and all bills on my own while taking care of a child full time.

Granite I am far from perfect and made bad decisions in the relationship as well, I never turned to social media for attention or to be petty and throw my relational problems to the world. Social media was the beginning of the end to our relationship, well that and Fortnite. It was an ongoing battle and constant arguments about me having to compete for attention and his priorities of being on his phone or on the game starting to increase. As time passed, compromises were disregarded and the communication between us decreased. I just got to the point where I accepted it for what is was because I had no other choice. With that said, I should've left 6 months into the relationship when I noticed he started getting more invested into the clout he was gaining in the cyber world than the real relationships he had surrounding him. #lessonlearned.

By this point, my insecurities were at an all-time high and he still gave no remorse or was willing to follow through on compromising after every time he got caught and me forgiving him. It was exactly what the saying is "Fool me once shame on you, fool me twice shame on me". These arising issues between Sam and I made me recognize that I have never been tested with repetitive situations in any of my past relationships nor did I know how to handle them especially dealing with this type of person.

Misery took over the relationship at this point no matter how much I met his love language, meeting mine was irrelevant to him because his priorities were focused towards cyber world, video games, and other women. It led to my fiancé meeting strangers and stepping out of the relationship by entertaining random women and talking to them inappropriately, which sometimes led to sexting. The last straw was when he organized to go to a female's house to hook up with her after he got off from Ubering that particular evening.

    I feel being a woman we are expected to accept and forgive a man whenever he cheats on us because "that's just how men are", but men get the upper hand and it's the end of the world when a woman cheats and then she is categorized as a "hoe". As I have learned my many lessons the hard way, I truly believe that it's wrong for either parties to step out of their intimate relationship behind their significant others back and it shouldn't be praised in society. It all comes down to communication, honesty, and making the conscious effort that both parties needs are being met. There are so many different dynamics in relationships you never know everything there is to every relationship you are in because everyone is different and what may work for one person won't work for another.

It has forced me to learn how to stand up for myself when it comes down to him and his mother, I consistently underwent verbal abuse, I was exposed to the feeling of being undervalued and manipulated for this person to get what he wanted. That relationship is what led me down the path of starting the EMDR therapy and learning about the real roots of my struggles.

Sam has admitted that he battles with anger issues and other mental triumphs. Those traits were idle once we first got together, then the colors came out of both of us once we started getting into arguments. He was good at provoking me and I was good at retaliating. I am a problem solver he is a grudge holder that likes to drag out issues and hold onto them until the end of time. He always held me at high standard, but mastered being a hypocrite and manipulator.

At first, I didn't see it, but as time went on I started noticing his patterns of always putting the blame on me and not taking responsibility for anything. He would often bring up past issues that had nothing to do with the current situation at hand so he could continue to argue. I came to accept that he has severe victim mentality and has struggles taking accountability for his own actions, which is very common.

Before this relationship or any relationship at that my brain had begun to tell itself to believe that I am unlovable, and when Sam came into the equation, he continuously validated that. I believed that I was never good enough no matter how hard I tried or what I did. I knew I just wanted to be loved so badly by this person that I was willing to go against my own beliefs and morals and even found myself apologizing for things that I hadn't wrongfully done just so he wouldn't get upset with me. I found myself once again in a place where I was when all I wanted was love and acceptance from both my father and step father, but how is a girl supposed to stand up for how she is supposed be treated by a man if she never had a positive example growing up from her father figures. So eventually verbal arguments escalated into throwing things and mild physical abuse. This person brought out anger and rage that I have never had to overcome before in any relationship, that is when I knew I couldn't be in it anymore and had to get out before one of us ended up brutally injured or dead.

Even though I started attending counseling sessions regularly and confronting my issues that I had been holding onto, Sam was still holding onto past situations and continuously brought them up whenever he had the opportunity. It defeated the purpose of me going to counseling to do the work in order to move forward in my life and grow mentally and spiritually. In order to be able to move past any disagreements I had to learn to change the way I communicated with this person, but that still didn't work.

Regardless of what I tried it was always the blame game and no resolutions were being made. As toxic and unloving as this situation was, it was impossible for me to let him go because all I wanted was his love and approval and I felt like once I got that it would've been a life accomplishment for me. I was so committed that it came to a point where we got engaged and were planning on getting married. The first relationship I had been in that lasted over a year and I allowed myself to let my wall down with this person and experience that vulnerable side that was foreign to me.

It became hard for me to respect Sam as much as I loved him, he pushed me to a point where I pitied him , but I knew that he is my daughter's father and no matter how I felt about him I could never come in between their relationship, especially since he wanted to continue being in her life. After all I wouldn't have been able to give birth to my beautiful little girl without him, and now I get to contribute towards making an impact on the future generations and get the opportunity to implement morals and values in my daughter that are lacking in the quality of humans today.

Thankfully, I am finally establishing and maintaining a stable and healthy balance in my life where I am being forced to process those long drawn out issues and gain closure and peace with each held on memory where I can finally embrace self-love within myself. The biggest secret was learning to create boundaries with those individuals that are opportunist and only care about themselves. By doing that I have started to attract people in my life where they are always so supportive and uplifting, even when I am at my worst, they force themselves in my life. The thing I am most grateful for is that they know me so well that they force themselves through the door to be there for me. It is hard to find friends that genuinely care without any motives and you both gain something out of the relationship.

7.

The Big Break Up

November 13, 2018

"Dear Diary,
I'm shutting down and urging to run away. I know he won't stop me. I know if someone is about me they would fight for me and this relationship. I'm so tired of begging for attention and other needs from someone that genuinely doesn't want to do it. My heart is to fragile and I'm to much of a unique woman who is desired by so many type of men to be strung along by someone who thinks he wants a family, but can't give up the single mindset including the self-centeredness. At this point all he cares about is himself. Do people like that ever change? It's hard to respect him as a man because he is lacking the attributes. I just want to be loved by one person. I want him to see me, know me, protect me, and me vulnerable with me. But apparently that is too much to ask for from men these days."

-Larissa Clark

The Big Break Up

The person I learned to love most had finally pushed me to my breaking point and I was done; regardless of my financial situation I knew that I couldn't be treated this way anymore and keeping my sanity for the sake of my daughter was more important to me than ending my life because of this person.

Late one evening in April of 2019 I came across a conversation that Sam was having in real time with this female planning what they were going to do to each other after he got done with work that evening. I was done. I was done dismissing his continuous broken promises he made me, I was done with him finding any opportunity to verbally abuse me in any disagreement we got into, I was done being second to his social media and his Xbox addiction, and I was done being overlooked when it came to expressing my feelings and concerns as if I was talking to a brick wall that just sat there smirking all the time and nodding it's head throughout the conversation. And in return it was a waste of time because there was no resolution. Instead, he gained enjoyment from belittling me.

It's not his fault though growing up he wasn't taught how to treat a woman, and everyone has always enabled this type of behavior his whole life with no consequences. I knew I should've left when he spent all of my daughter's college money on traveling to try to establish his modeling career and his leisure expenses because he would rather play video games than create ways to make money, but I gave him the benefit of the doubt and even though he didn't show remorse I still forgave him.

Now that he got caught for the fifth time trying to organize a hook up session with a female I WAS DONE. I texted the girl told her she could have him and he will be showing up with his suitcase and Xbox. After being called a crazy bitch by this dumb girl I started packing his suitcase and when he found out I knew his response was, "why are you going through my stuff?" Once again. no remorse. And according to him I was the one in the wrong.

That was the moment I felt most alone, irrelevant, and just a piece of tossed meat to the side from someone that supposedly loves me and wants to spend the rest of their life with me. I told him go stay with the girl he had been arranging to sleep with; of course, he hurried and rushed home. He came back to the house in a rage but was only mad because he got caught and that I was finally putting my foot down. He was so mad that he attempted to take my little girl with him during late hours of the night with nowhere to go. I was standing in between her bed and him, so he forcefully pushed me to get me out of the way so he could grab her just to prove his point.

Thankfully I had called my two best friends to come over before he got there because I knew this situation wasn't going to end very good with it being jus the two of us alone in that level of anger and would escalade to physical destruction like it had a couple days prior to.

It's unfortunate that both my friends had to be there and witness the ugliness and be a part of it, but Alayna stayed safe and was able to go back to sleep and Sam got escorted off the premises by a couple of officers. I held on so tight to my little girl that night when she was sleeping, I then experienced a glimpse of how it feels to get your child taken away from you and not knowing what's going to happen.

I am grateful for my girlfriend spending the night with me that night and comforting me, I couldn't have gone through that situation alone and that is why it is so important to have support who will be there for you in your darkest moments and protect you when you can't protect yourself.

When I reflect back on that incident what I find funniest about that whole situation is that he still went to the girl's house that night because he had nowhere to go and was feeling sorry for himself because he got caught and was facing the consequences. When he left for good, I felt a sigh of relief and a huge dark weight lifted off my shoulders. I am glad God took matters into his hands and forced things to happen the way they did because I kept making excuses for myself on why I shouldn't leave just yet even though things kept getting worse and worse to the point where I was broken and losing my sanity and on the brink of taking my life and leaving my daughter behind without her mother.

By that point I was manic depressed, and therapy wasn't helping because as soon as I got home, I was in that toxic environment which sent my mental state of mind backwards instead of forward, which made living, breathing, and even existing in this world challenging. Whenever I brought to Sam's attention how the phase of the relationship was affecting my mental health and was putting me in a bad headspace, he would just mimic me as if my self-awareness on my mental health was a joke.

Now that he is gone for good, what was I supposed to do now? How do I pick up the broken pieces? How am I going to afford all of my bills alone being a single mom? Who am I? What's my purpose? Am I that damaged? Ugh I miss him, don't call him.

This was the moment I found myself desperately needing God to give me the strength and guidance on what to do next. I lost the love of my life, the parent assistance, the financial help, who I was, and what my purpose was in life. I had no idea what to do or where to go at this point or even what I was supposed to do next.

A job opportunity presented itself in Denver that summer, where I could leave and work in a different state for 10 days. This was my chance to be in a safe place to regain both my mental and physical health and spend time with my little girl while being around people that loved me.

Being fresh out of a relationship with my daughter's father was so confusing for me. I was going through the grieving phases as if someone died: anger, hurt, sadness, resentment, denial, hope. While on this month-long journey I had to relearn to love myself and forgive my daughters father for continuously hurting me mentally, verbally, and physically.

During that month there was a lot of silence and a lot of music, a lot of crying, a lot of praying for strength and guidance, and a lot of adventure. Even during that time, it was a struggle for me to take interest in men, which of course I figured was normal because I found interest focusing on my career and loving on my little girl. I was loving on myself as well by giving myself all the time to heal and find my true inner peace, so I turned it over to God and let him take the reins.

The Big Break Up

I knew I grew when I didn't resort to my normal alcohol and sex habits to cope with my trauma, I was sober most of the time embracing the pain and working through it as difficult as it was. Sam was in and out of the picture after I came back from my eat, pray, love journey and it was still a rocky road. There was still no consistency and we couldn't see eye to eye on things, but I was learning to stand up for myself towards him and create boundaries.

I was evolving into a new peaceful place in my life where I was eliminating and decreasing the things that caused me the most anxiety and challenged my beliefs by setting boundaries on all my relationships. My anxiety attacks decreased dramatically, and I was finally gaining back an appetite where I could enjoy a meal again because of the change in my environment and the people I had surrounding me.

In order to stay on that road and continue this positive journey I had to learn to let go and surrender all of my demons that I was holding onto with guilt.

The most needed factor that has helped me get through this past year's hardships aside from God and therapy, was the emotional support I had from my true friends and mom, who went the extra mile to step up and help me get back on my feet. me. They always took the time to listen and give suggestions, constantly reached out to check on me, they were very supportive and uplifting, and even helped with watching my little girl. I will give the most credit to my mom, who has been my biggest support in the most time of need. Even though she is far away she has helped me tremendously, emotionally, spiritually, and financially when it came to my daughter. Even though we may have our own differences between our own relationship she has been there for me, even more than Sam has when it came down to meeting all of my daughter's needs and well-being. And for that I am truly grateful for her and it motivates me to be the biggest support my daughter has in her corner as she grows up, like my mother is to me.

One of my close girlfriends helped me come to the realization of how terrified I am to be loved and treated the way I believe I should be treated by a man and instead tolerate childlike behavior in order for my daughter to have a relationship with her father.

Eventually, I came to the realization that I was doing it all wrong and wasn't making God the center of my core and putting faith in the higher power, but instead making man the center of my core and putting faith in him, which is why it was so dysfunctional. I believe everything happens as it supposed to, but sometimes God steps into situations to handle them for me when I am not capable of following through on my own.

I've learned a lot from witnessing my mom and so many mothers raise their children on their own with fathers doing the bare minimum and it makes me angry and resentful because I would never want my daughter to go through the pain and heartache on top of being another statistic just like I was. I don't want my child's father to be in the system just like so many men in this nation are. I don't want to be another statistic and be a single mother raising her daughter alone and struggling to find love because I am paranoid to bring men around my little girl. NO ONE should ever have to go through this experience.

When I filed for child support originally, I was dead set on the path I had to take in order to hold that person accountable to take care of his child since he wasn't doing it willingly and It was a struggle taking care of our child and finances alone, my spirit was very bothered that I felt obligated to go this route. Even though my anxiety was out of the roof and I couldn't think straight; I had to take a step back and realize that my spirit was able to find peace with the situation because focused my attention on what made the most rational sense.

    I haven't been in a court room since I was going through my seven-day trial facing my stepdad. I feel people don't realize the nuanced ways in which trauma can impact your life. On that day, my anxiety was through the roof to the point where I could not think and all I could hear was my heart pounding out of my chest. I was able to walk out of the building getting the results I came for, but I was so discombobulated everything was a blur and I had no idea what we agreed upon. I get so frustrated because having a mature relationship, we should be able to choose one another. Why is it so hard for both sides to make the effort to work through our own personal issues and relationship issues in order to continue a healthy family dynamic?

The Big Break Up

Taking it one day at a time I have been learning my value and embracing my self-worth especially after we broke up and viewing myself as much more than he or any man has ever made me believe I am. What a toxic situation to be in that was ongoing and I couldn't get out of. It was so hard to walk away from that abusive relationship because I genuinely loved that person, I continued to give him a benefit of the doubt that he would wake up and change his ways and love me the way I deserved to be loved because I loved him. In reality as time was passing by that verbal abuse from a narcist led me to believe that I was the problem and everything that happened in our relationship was my fault and I caused this to happen.

I'm very appreciative that I went through this experience because I made it out alive and with a better mindset than where I was when I went into the relationship. This relationship forced me to confront my issues that I brought in with me and made me realize I came into the relationship not happy with myself and not loving who I was. I was taught to walk away when I see the red flags and that I should not give my energy into someone who is going to treat me less than.

8.

Becoming a Mom & Living with Trauma

August 17, 2017

*"Dear Diary,
I fear for the future and what is in store. I put my full faith in God and know that everything that will happen was because he wanted and created it to be. Just because people may be ugly towards me doesn't mean I get out of character; I will continue to be who I am. I love me and I accept me. I know it's hard for people to understand me and that is okay I've accepted that, but I am one of a kind and I will leave a stamp in this world when I'm gone."*

-Larissa Clark

Being a parent isn't for everyone, it certainly wasn't something that I was sure about. Growing up in a big family and being the oldest didn't motivate me to want a big family as well. I was an only child until I was eight years old, which resulted in being raised with an "only child" syndrome so, the idea of having children wasn't that amusing to me. Until I found out I was 5 weeks pregnant a week before my high school graduation. I wasn't as invincible as I thought I was.

When I found out I was at a loss of words and reality set in that I had life changing decisions to make that would affect my future drastically, especially not knowing how to tell my mom. I have always idolized my mother and respected her as the woman she is. She is such a caring and selfless individual who will give you the clothes off her back no matter what the situation is, and she is so forgiving.

I've always admired that she is not one to hold grudges and moves forward from situations versus holding onto situations and bring them up later down the line. Regardless of her nature, I was so scared to tell her because I didn't know what she would think of me, so it became one of my biggest kept secrets and still is to certain people till this day.

My then-boyfriend who was 2 years younger than me wanted me to go through with the pregnancy and was so excited. I felt the opposite; I was terrified and felt alone because no one else wanted what I wanted, which some would call me selfish, but I was 18 years old and didn't want to bring a child into this world knowing I'd resent it and hating it for being another person taking my life away again.

My mom found out shortly afterward, without me having to tell her. When it came down to her confronting me, I had to confess. Of course, she wasn't happy because I was about to graduate high school and go off to college in Houston. She was very graceful and nonjudgmental with the situation being at hand. She encouraged me to go through with the pregnancy and offered the opportunity to continuing to stay with her while I worked and went to college classes in the evening and during the day I could help take care of my siblings while taking care of the child.

As kind-hearted and problem solving as she was, I didn't want that for myself and knowing that I would have the resentment towards a child who didn't ask to be brought into this world. I made a promise to myself, when moving forward from this situation I would continue my life and achieve whatever goals I set for myself and fulfill my life visions.

    I found a local clinic that had financial assistance for people that weren't in a financially stable situation and I was able to schedule an appointment. I followed through with termination of the pregnancy the day after my graduation. My dad never knew about the abortion and still doesn't till this day. I was embarrassed to tell him because I knew I would be a disappointment in his eyes even more than I already was and felt like he would hate me for an eternity. My relationship with my then-boyfriend ended shortly after leaving for college, but initially my abortion broke us up. As for my mom, our relationship shifted after finding out what I decided to do and not telling her about it.

Till this very day only a handful of people knew about what happened because people are so judgmental and opinionated when it comes to a woman getting an abortion, but the few people that did know were very supportive and understanding of my decision. I was once an 18-year-old girl who felt alone and ashamed for what I did.

I was so scared that if anyone knew what I did I would be dismissed and disowned, especially when it came to the Catholic Church and any other religion. The things I must be silenced about is daunting to me because it isn't accepted by society or makes people uncomfortable. What's even worse is that these sensitive topics such as rape, abortion, prostitution, alcoholism, etc. can't be discussed around the people who are closest to me, literally "my blood family". These are everyday issues that need to be discussed the most, especially in the younger generations.

Today I'm breaking that silence. I made a drastic, selfish decision and it was one of the best decisions in my life. I'll never forget my mother telling me I would regret getting an abortion and would most likely get pregnant again because of the guilt. She was wrong! I wasn't ready to bring a child into this world and take care of it mentally and physically, but it was also a life lesson and I never put myself in that situation again. This is an example of how I have learned to take ownership of my own decisions and life.

What forced me to take that big step to start processing and regurgitate my internal issues in order for them to not affect my present life was becoming a mom. My fiancé and I had talked somewhat about the idea of having a baby, and we were open to it until we started fighting constantly. True colors were starting to come out and I lost interest in wanting a child with him. Then I found out I was pregnant Memorial Day weekend 2017! SURPRISE!!

This time, I believed I was in a place in my life to bear a child and bring one into the world. My fiancé was ecstatic. I was very afraid because I didn't know what was in store for me, and I was about to be stuck with this guy for the rest of my life. Well, too late for second guessing now.

Pregnancy wasn't easy for me mentally and physically because of my PTSD. My anxiety was uncontrollable, and I had no coping mechanism. I wasn't going to therapy in the most hormonal time of the pregnancy and ended up spiraling into deep depression. For the first three months of my pregnancy, I found myself locking myself in the closet hyperventilating anytime Sam and I argued. I hated it so much, I couldn't resort to my bad habits, no drugs, emotionless sex, alcohol. On top of that I was getting pressure from people around me because of how much weight I was losing even though I couldn't control it and wasn't doing it on purpose.

My mind went down the rabbit hole and at first the thoughts were aborting my child. I made a promise to myself so I couldn't go through with it, then my thoughts progressed in contemplating taking my own life and I was starting to lose myself in the process again. I felt like I didn't have anyone I could confide in because they would just judge me and use how I was feeling in that moment against me down the line, (which happened to me anyway).

It was one of the most significant challenges in life that I had to overcome – my PTSD was uncontrollable due to the raging hormones, and I couldn't take it anymore and decided to seek counseling, which is when I started working with my former therapist. While it was a low point for me, it was a major turning point in my life. As they say: "It's darkest before the dawn."

I hope that anyone that is reading this provides support to anyone that tells you something is wrong with them. Be someone to reach out to – especially if they are pregnant and hormonal believe them.

The biggest struggle in my pregnancy was not having the emotional support from my partner that I needed with the fragile state of mind I was in. I fought through and stayed consistent with my therapy, which Sam thought was a joke that I was going because in his eyes nothing was wrong with me. I know I have tried committing suicide on a couple of occasions, but I felt like I was more willing in that state than when I wasn't pregnant. It didn't help having an unsupportive partner who couldn't empathize with me being hormonal and battling PTSD demons, let alone both combined.

Overall, once I found my therapist and started attending therapy sessions on a weekly basis, we were able to establish healthy coping mechanisms such as deep breathing, grounding, working out, journaling, meditating, and more. There was a window where she highly recommended anxiety and depression medication, but I declined because I didn't want to be on it while I was pregnant and wanted to work through my emotions using a holistic approach.

With all the changes I was going through physically, mentally, spiritually, and not knowing the unknown gave me even more anxiety. So, my therapist directed my focus on things that I had control over in order to help decrease the anxiety and encouraged me to channel my energy into activities I enjoy that make me feel good.

What ultimately helped my depression throughout the pregnancy was learning healthy coping skills that kept my interest such as; finding more ways to laugh, listen to music louder, journaling, being around people that were supportive, eating healthy foods and increasing my meal intake, and working out daily and staying fit.

One thing I could always control throughout my life was my weight and how I looked physically. My therapist helped me recognize that by me controlling my weight and how I looked was the only control I had while going through the abuse, even though I was skinny throughout my childhood. Until, I started getting older and physically developing that's when the boys started paying attention to me, which made me feel good. It was my safety net. What kept me sane and still feel like I had control over something in my life, was my weight and how I physically looked.

So, the weight gain alone throughout pregnancy was a struggle. The first 3 months of my pregnancy I had no appetite and couldn't eat. It got to a point where I was losing so much weight because I wasn't hungry and struggled eating. Instead I was drinking protein smoothies and fruit smoothies religiously in order to get the nutrients that I needed. I also struggled with the thought of gaining too much weight and losing my sculpted figure. I became obsessed with working out and eating healthy foods once I gained a decent appetite. I managed to only gain 15 pounds by the end of my pregnancy and never had to buy maternity clothes or have any stretch marks.

So, my method was a success story and my depression didn't completely take over because I was still able to have that control throughout my pregnancy.

When the big day came, Sam was walking out the door to head to work early Sunday morning and I ended up driving myself to the hospital to check myself into the labor and delivery unit. The nurse at the check in desk was so confused why I was there, but I let them know I was having bad cramping and thought I was in labor. After all those years of horror stories I had heard about hours of labor, mine was the complete opposite. My delivery was very unique– it was fast and smooth with no tears or cuts. The doctors said I didn't even need an epidural because of how fast the labor had progressed. I was up and walking in my normal clothes by that evening. My doctors told me that I helped my body by staying fit, ate a healthy diet, and was continuously active during my pregnancy.

My beautiful girl made her way into the world healthy and looking like a Chinese porcelain doll with fine dark brunette hair and grey eyes. Sam and I decided to name her Alayna. It's originated in the Middle East, which is some of my ethnic background. We named her middle name after my great-grandmother's first name. My daughter is now a legacy she is the only girl of 5th generation of women and that gave me something to look forward to throughout my whole pregnancy. I am thankful that my great-grandmother stayed alive to witness that historic day. She was so happy and so proud to be a first time great-great grandmother of 5 generations of women.

Alayna is the epitome of my world because she is such a small little person who continues to touch so many lives with the unique personality she has! She is very inquisitive and curious; she catches on to everything instantly, she challenges my teaching techniques and parenting styles. She is my musical, free-spirited child. When I was pregnant, I prayed and prayed that she would look like her daddy and inherit my intelligence and personality traits, which she did. I couldn't have asked for any child greater than what God has given me with, I believe that *saying God never gives you more than you can handle*, and I agree with that saying 110%. He knew what I needed when it came to my child's qualities.

As I start to age in my years, I become more aware of how important the quality of life is, and how often this concept gets taken for granted. Throughout the course of my life I have always felt that there was an expectation that I had to live up to, like there is a rulebook that I get pressured to follow in many different categories. But looking at who I am today, I by nature don't fall into those routines, and I will continue to live my life freely and abundantly because I lived in a routine the first half of my life as a prisoner. The amount of growth I have I experienced spiritually and mentally has been substantially more within the past 6 months than in my whole 27 years.

As I am continuing to learn through my own journey, it's my mission to be the positive role model for Alayna as I want to be for anyone else. My vision is to allow God to use me to help people in any way possible and to fulfill my purpose of life. By reading a glimpse of my life journey, I hope that I can be an influence on why it's important to establish and maintain a healthy mind, healthy relationships, and overall a healthy you.

I Could Be Worse

[About Author]

Larissa's journey as an advocate for sexual & domestic abuse awareness started in 2012. Because of her strength and courage, Larissa has won multiple awards and has been given opportunities to tell her story nationwide.

    Throughout the years she has gained experience and exposure through being the founder of multiple companies, including Larissa's Books.

    Traveling to new places, learning about different cultures, and enjoying exotic food has helped Larissa learn who she is and find inner peace from all the triumphs she has had to overcome.

    She is determined to help others who are faced with similar challenges and situations. As she continues to write books, Larissa promotes self-growth, spiritual finding, healthy coping mechanisms, and encouraging every reader to find peace in their walk of life.

When purchasing the paperback book, a portion of the proceeds will go to a victim's advocacy center called Sunflower House located in Shawnee, KS.
To find out more information on the organization please visit:
www.sunflowerhouse.org

www.ingramcontent.com/pod-product-compliance
Lightning Source LLC
Chambersburg PA
CBHW032258150426
43195CB00008BA/499